BEI GRIN MACHT SICH IHR WISSEN BEZAHLT

- Wir veröffentlichen Ihre Hausarbeit, Bachelor- und Masterarbeit

- Ihr eigenes eBook und Buch - weltweit in allen wichtigen Shops

- Verdienen Sie an jedem Verkauf

Jetzt bei www.GRIN.com hochladen und kostenlos publizieren

GRIN

Development of the E-Court System in the Dark Era of Pakistan

Aijaz Ahmed

GRIN ☺

Bibliografische Information der Deutschen Nationalbibliothek:

Die Deutsche Nationalbibliothek verzeichnet diese Publikation in der Deutschen Nationalbibliografie; detaillierte bibliografische Daten sind im Internet über http://dnb.d-nb.de abrufbar.

ISBN: 9783346918710
Dieses Buch ist auch als E-Book erhältlich.

© GRIN Publishing GmbH
Trappentreustraße 1
80339 München

Druck und Bindung: Books on Demand GmbH, Norderstedt Germany
Gedruckt auf säurefreiem Papier aus verantwortungsvollen Quellen

Das Buch bei GRIN: https://www.grin.com/document/1379255

Development of the E-Court System in the Dark Era of Pakistan

Aijaz Ahmed

7/7/23

Ziauddin university faculty of Law, politics, & Governance

ABSTRACT

The E-court system is a modern approach to the judicial system in which online court proceedings take place. It has been developed in Pakistan more vastly post-covid 2019. The initiative took place as globally there was a pandemic going on which indulge people to follow the SOPS to deal with daily affairs which includes court litigation as well. This research study investigates the feasibility of incorporating e-courts into the Pakistani legal system as a step towards faster justice and peaceful growth. As it has been adopted globally and utilized across various jurisdictions a comparative analysis technique is utilized to examine the incorporation of e-courts into multiple other legal systems like India, Malaysia, Turkey, Canada, Azerbaijan, the United Kingdom, and the United States of America. The consequences of e-courts in these systems will be investigated and compared to Pakistan's judicial systems. The analysis will help to address multiple questions a reasonable person can think of regarding the e-court system. Technology is playing a vital role in resolving online dispute resolution (ODR); however, it is not fully developed due to the flaws and gaps between the technology and the law which is expected that within a few years would be filled and both would be standing on the same page. We recommend that an e-court system compliant with the Pakistani legal system be developed wisely according to the nature and urgency of the case.

Keywords: Electronic courts, Speedy justice, online proceedings, Pakistan legal system, Comparative Analysis, Online dispute resolution (ODR), Technology, Alternate Dispute resolution (ADR), ICT, video link, online proceedings.

INTRODUCTION

In the past few decades, the information and technology of communication (ICT) is playing a vital role in connecting people from any part of the world. Initially, people were more often found using it for socializing, e-commerce activities, online shopping, gaming, for educational purposes as well. After the pandemic, Covid-19 it changed the dynamics of ICT as it was more often and commonly being used by every age group people in all aspects. As it was witnessed in Pakistan educational institutes had started to educate students online through Zoom and Google Classrooms. This mode of educating the students was exercised all over the world with different names in India it was e-patshala and Swayam and in South Korea, it was Edmodo and Classln. The e-commerce activities were at their peak as it was lockdown all over the world and only online buying and selling could be done through Ali Baba and many more platforms like these to fulfill their basic need sitting in one place following the SOPs. Even the healthcare facilities were remote in the sense that a patient could see a doctor online through telehealth facilities in Pakistan Oldac and Marham.com was being used and in Brazil "Telemedicine for all" initiative was introduced to expand this facility. The working population was working remotely from homes through the Google meeting room facilities.

In the working population not only the business or private officials are included but also the government officials and more gladly even the judiciary has set up an e-court system. It was necessary to do so as "justice delayed is justice denied". All the activities were being conducted the same way as post-covid then how can there be no issues arising? And what about the issues which were ongoing before the pandemic? To remove uncertainty in the justice system the e-court system was expanded all over the world. The word **"expanded"** has been used instead of introduced as it was not a new way of availing justice however was being practiced less in different countries. In 1984, the first e-court was established in the state of Texas in the United States of America. On 9th May 2019 in a landmark case of the Supreme Court of Pakistan, the e-court system was established. The case was being heard in Islamabad and the Advocate was presenting it from Karachi through the video link connectivity. It was the first time in Pakistan a step towards the development of a judicial system was taken where civil cases could take up to 25 years and on an odd day can reach up to 70 years.

E-courts are electronic systems used in courtrooms to help with traditional courtroom procedures. These systems enable access to computers and distinct computer systems for showing electronic documents on screens to judges, parties involved, and court officers. The core electronic database in this system contains all the relevant information for quick access and retrieval. It permits efficient evidence searching and simplifies its showing or assessment. The paragraph emphasizes the significance of deploying first-generation E-court systems in nations with traditional court systems. This technology change intends to improve the justice system's accessibility, ease, and affordability. It recommends using numerous technical methods such as e-filing, e-trial with video links for remote testimony, and paperless electronic case management. As Justice Bleby pointed out, adopting electronic courts allows all parties concerned, including the trial judge and court employees, to securely access and handle essential materials both inside and outside the courtroom.

Pakistan has faced many challenges in the judicial system in terms of efficiency, transparency, and access to justice. According to the World Justice Project Rule of Law Index, 2021 ranked 130 out of 139 all around the world. The major reason behind the pending cases in Pakistan is due to the shortage of judges, court staff, and outdated management and legal proceeding. On a global scale, the use of technology in dispute settlement has received great recognition. Various judicial systems have recently implemented Online Dispute Resolution (ODR) as an alternate method of conflict resolution. This technical advancement offers a tremendous possibility to speed up the delivery of justice. The accessibility of justice can be improved by leveraging ODR and other technology means, providing better ease to individuals. The use of technology in legal procedures is now limited to specific fields such as electronic case filing, research, and case administration. However, the incorporation of technology into legal systems is becoming an unavoidable requirement, necessitating the creation of an Electronic Court (E-court) system to ensure the effective administration of justice.

The resolution of cases by judges without the physical presence of key parties is one component of the E-court system. Arguments and evidence are given before judges via video links, and judgments are delivered via an online platform. The E-court system works in parallel with existing court structures, providing a framework innovation aimed at increasing the accessibility, convenience, and affordability of court services. The basic notion is to keep the existing court system while incorporating technological advances to deliver services that extend beyond the constraints of a typical courtroom. This hybrid approach promotes the administration of justice by utilizing modern technologies, making access to justice easier for litigants while also solving the issue of case delay that now affects our court system.

Research Questions

1) Are the people of Pakistan aware of the E-court system?
2) Is Pakistan's E-court system maintaining its standards of it as compared to other countries E-courts?
3) Is the E-court system in Pakistan suitable for all types of cases?
4) Is there any effect of the E-court system on litigation in Pakistan?
5) Is Pakistan's E-court system a biased way of availing justice?
6) Is the weightage of pros more over the cons of the E-court system in Pakistan?

LITERATURE REVIEW

The Supreme Court of Pakistan faces a record backlog of 48,594 cases due to the Covid-19 pandemic. To improve transparency, the court has proposed a video link mechanism, requiring each courtroom or bench to have a Wi-Fi-connected cell phone and applications like Skype, WhatsApp, and Telegram. In May 2019 and the provision of video-link facilities for advocates in Karachi, Lahore, Peshawar, and Quetta were initiated. However, the current infrastructure of the court system does not permit the use of technology in most cases. This proposal aims to maintain transparency, openness, and mirror the court cell phone screen on television sets. Advocate Khurram Chughtai believes the restrictions on video link hearings at the registry are flawed, and courts have rapidly adopted digital technologies during the pandemic. Virtual hearings are expected to improve transparency, efficiency, and the implementation of Article 37-d of the constitution, ensuring inexpensive and expeditious justice. (Hasnat Malik 2021).

The coronavirus has severely impacted governments worldwide, leading to rising unemployment, debt, and broken economies. The court system and access to justice have been a concern, with Pakistan's prisons facing mass overcrowding and poor hygiene conditions. The country's prisons have a backlog of cases, with 43,847 cases pending until March 31st. The Covid-19 lockdown has further exacerbated the issue, with many under-trial prisoners waiting for their cases to proceed. Online court proceedings are a potential solution to the problem, as they are crucial for maintaining order, stability, and accountability during unstable times. Pakistan has already implemented e-court systems in its Supreme Court and overseas courts, with advocates arguing cases through video links. However, to fully implement an online court system, drastic steps need to be taken, including efficient mechanisms for online filing, uploading documents, signing, e-stamps, and arguments.

Countries like the US, Canada, and Turkey have implemented online court systems, with Turkey having a national electronic service across all judicial functions. Under lockdown, the UK Supreme Court conducts entire cases by video link, while the US adopts a virtual court system. An online court system could significantly improve access to justice for vulnerable minority groups and women, streamlining court proceedings and potentially easing the backlog of cases. The process of digitizing courts is challenging, but if courts are not able to maintain stability during these times of instability, who will? (Sadaf Shahzad 2020).

The Islamabad High Court (IHC) has been adapting to the changing conditions of the pandemic by using modern technology to ensure that judges infected with the virus could safely conduct proceedings while isolating at home. Justice Mian gul Hassan Aurangzeb, who contracted the novel coronavirus, went into self-isolation at home and presided over cases assigned to him. The IHC staff arranged for hearings to be held, allowing Justice Aurangzeb to connect via video link to lawyers and litigants in the courtroom. This allowed Justice Aurangzeb to present their arguments as normal. The court had already made provisions for technology to bridge distances during the pandemic via E-courts, allowing lawyers and litigants who may be infected or unable to travel to appear before the bench in important cases. The lawyers' community has welcomed the move, as it will help keep not only judges but also lawyers and litigants safe during the pandemic. It is admirable that the court is making an attempt to stay up with contemporary technology; the change is anticipated to enhance the judicial system and do rid of pointless delays. (Saqib Bashir 2020).

At both the national and international levels, technology has had a huge influence on how we live our everyday lives. Globalization and rapid technological advancement have generated new chances and challenges for every industry to advance. Information has impacted the judiciary developing a hybrid court system that fuses conventional judicial procedures with contemporary technologies, such as information and communication technology. In a number of industrialized and emerging nations, including Malaysia, the E-court system, which integrates electronic papers, filing fees, court notices, and court information, has been put into place. The goal of the electronic court system is to provide swift, reasonable, and fair justice. Due to Pakistan's low judge-to-citizen ratio and huge case backlog, a hybrid system is required in order to speed up justice for far-flung and underprivileged residents. Due to a lack of technology infrastructure and internet connectivity during the epidemic and lockdown, Pakistan's court has encountered difficulties. The Islamabad High Court and the Lahore High Court have implemented an online case management system, making the judicial system more practical, economical, and serviceable.

However, Pakistan faces hurdles in implementing the e-court system, such as lawyers going on strike for their own gain. Delaying justice to the victim is a violation of fundamental human rights, and e-courts can be a game changer in increasing transparency, enhancing justice dispensation, saving government resources, decreasing public spending, and creating jobs opportunities for skilled workers. (Abida Naureen and Asadullah 2023).

The COVID-19 pandemic has hindered the judiciary's ability to dispense justice, leading to a lack of technological capacity in subordinate and high courts. The Access to Justice Program in 2002 has not transformed courts' functioning, but digital transformation could help emerge as a leader in public service delivery and create a conducive investment climate. High courts in Kerala, Bombay, and Calcutta have adopted Zoom video conferencing for hearings. The Supreme Court of the United States has embraced digital technology and universal access to mobile connectivity, implementing e-filing, e-disposal, hearings, and e-governance. E-filing offers smart identification, reduced paper usage, and automatic allocation to relevant courts. E-hearing usage has increased since 2020 due to work-from-home policies and lockdowns. Video conferencing is already used by the Supreme Court in all registries and some civil courts, providing a safe environment for deposing evidence and cross-examination. However, digital transformation faces risks, including systemic changes, technical risks, and illiteracy. (Asma Hamid 2020).

Technology has significantly transformed our interactions and interactions, making access to justice more convenient and accessible. E-courts, synchronous with traditional court systems, are designed to make court services accessible, convenient, and affordable. These hybrid systems make use of cutting-edge technology to streamline court operations and shorten case pending times, including first-generation E-courts and AI-based systems. The E-courts system, which dates back to the late 1980s, allows parties, trial judges, and court personnel safe access to court materials. The idea first appeared in the late 1980s, when video connections were made available during court proceedings. E-filing in the E-courts system in Malaysia developed as a result of the start of the E-government in 1997. Since the year 2000, Australia's courts have also been utilizing technology, with an emphasis on enhancing its efficacy and efficiency. Increased digital displays of complicated evidence, live transcription, video connection technology, and digital recording have all been made possible by the digital searchable system. The Case Management System (CMS), electronic filing, and online record keeping are just a few of the substantial improvements that the e-Court system has made to the Chinese judicial system. While online record-keeping makes it simple to monitor performance and retrieve information, e-filing makes communication and filing more efficient. Due to their shared history of colonialism and the laws they both inherited Pakistan and India have comparable judicial systems. The Indian and Malaysian e-court systems share a pyramid structure, with the Supreme Court and High Courts being the highest courts. The increasing population in India and Pakistan has led to an overburdening judiciary, violating constitutional and human rights. However, online dispute resolution has several disadvantages compared to traditional methods. One major issue is the connectivity issue, which can make recording personal statements or advocating arguments challenging. Legal professionals must implement e-courts responsibly, as the system creates an electronic record that may infringe on other parties' rights. The E-Court System aims to make justice universal, portable, and available while boosting investor confidence and the economy. (Dr. Muhammad Asif khan and Babar Ali 2021)

Access to justice is crucial in judicial systems worldwide, and information communication and technology (ICT) is being considered as a potential instrument for expeditious justice delivery. E-courts, which are expeditious systems of adjudication, have been established in developed and developing countries. In Pakistan, ICT has been a step forward towards modern reforms in the legal system, with the Supreme Court aiming to institute e-court proceedings using ICT. The Pakistani justice system has made significant strides in digitalization, with advanced case management systems and video conferencing for expedited justice delivery. The Case Management System (CMS) is crucial for enhancing the efficiency of E-courts in Pakistan, improving service efficiency, streamlining legal services, and ensuring quality, transparency, and public accountability. Training programs for judges, lawyers, and staff are necessary for systematically evolving e-courts. (Zeeshan Ashraf Qureshi 2021).

The COVID-19 pandemic has significantly impacted Pakistan's dispute resolution process, with courts, mediators, arbitrators, and lawyers adapting to e-technologies for processes they would never have considered not doing in person. Video-conferencing applications like Zoom have seen a 76% increase in usage in recent weeks. The E-court, launched in the Supreme Court of Pakistan in 2019, aims to resolve long delays in cases before courts. Pakistan should continue to use video-conferencing applications to save time and costs, as well as avoid the environmental impact of traveling to meetings. A key agreement that tries to ensure the effective application of technology in arbitration procedures is the Seoul Protocol on Video Conferencing in International Arbitration. There are nine articles in the Protocol, including ones on witness examination, the location for videoconferencing, observers, documents, technical requirements, test conferencing, audio-conferencing backup, interpretation, recording, and preliminary arrangements. However, challenges to arbitral awards may arise due to insufficient online hearings or technical difficulties. In Pakistan, the pro-arbitration stance should address these concerns in a fair and practical manner, balancing the parties' rights and bringing the application up to date with the times. For Pakistan's courts and arbitrators, the Seoul Protocol on Video Conferencing in International Arbitration is a useful tool for navigating the difficulties of online arbitration and ensuring the efficient operation of the legal system. (Dr. Tariq Mahmood 2020).

Efficiency, openness, and access to justice are issues with Pakistan's judicial system. The nation has a backlog of almost 2.1 million cases, which contributes to its low ranking in the World Justice Project Index. A scarcity of judges, inadequate court personnel, obsolete case management systems, and drawn-out legal processes are some of the issues causing this backlog. For the benefit of litigants, judges, attorneys, and court personnel, digital technology integration may considerably increase efficiency and transparency in judicial operations. This may improve underprivileged populations' access to the judicial system. The US, UK, and EU are examples of international best practices that have effectively integrated technological efforts into their judicial processes. The High Court of Sindh in Pakistan has embraced technological innovations including real-time case management, video conferencing, e-Court centers, smartphone apps, and online methods for posting bail bonds and paying fines. But obstacles prevent Pakistan from integrating technology. These include a lack of digital literacy among judges, attorneys, and court employees, resource abuse, a dearth of training programs, and inadequate infrastructure upgrades. Potential solutions to these issues include fostering digital literacy among legal experts and court personnel as well as investing in human resources, training programs, diversity, and inclusiveness. (Marvi Qazi 2023).

Digital court systems are being used more often, which has increased interest in e-justice and the World Development Report's "Digital Dividends." The use of computer-assisted transcription, digital audio systems, and audio/visual (A/V) recordings in electronic court reporting has the potential to enhance judge performance in a variety of situations. Kenya, Malaysia, Singapore, Romania, Croatia, and other nations are implementing e-reporting systems using a variety of techniques. E-reporting has benefits such as promoting civil conduct, boosting efficiency, enhancing transparency and accountability, reducing corruption or misuse of the legal system, and expanding access to justice. E-recording has disadvantages, too, such being expensive, time-consuming, and needing constant upkeep. Additionally, not all technology is created equal, and qualified personnel are needed to effectively manage the technology. Stenographers, according to certain courts, provide quicker, more accurate, and more affordable alternatives than electronic systems. It is critical to research which choices give the most value for money and are most likely to enhance the effectiveness and standard of justice as courts consider the best options for automating the judicial process. (Georgia Harley and Agnes Said 2018).

The Pakistani criminal justice system needs reforms to uphold the rule of law and ensure equality for all individuals. The Electronic Transaction Ordinance, 2002 (ETO) was promulgated to address the increasing importance of digital evidence in civil and criminal trials. The ordinance declared electronic or digital evidence to be primary and affirmed the originality of electronic documents, information, records, and transactions. Digital evidence is now used in the prosecution of all types of crimes, not just e-crime. Pakistan's legal regime gives admissibility to digital evidence in the form of modern and technical devices, with Articles 59 and 164 dealing with digital evidence. The amendments in ETO confirm the admissibility of digital evidence, but they do not specify the weight or value of evidence. Pakistani courts should provide guidance on how to make digital evidence admissible, as everything is not written in the law. Guidelines for authenticity, reliability, and originality of digital evidence have been developed by American Law Reports and UK police Chiefs. The amendments to the Pakistan Evidence Standards (QSO) since ETO 2002 focus on the admissibility of evidence rather than its weight or value. Pakistani courts have begun to prioritize probative value over the admissibility of digital evidence. To address the issue of digital evidence admissibility, Pakistan must establish rules and regulations regarding custody, storage, authenticity, and reliability of digital evidence, establish a precedent for relying on digital evidence as the sole evidence for a conviction, appoint an expert in the digital world to assist the court in analyzing digital evidence, prepare an expert team in each district to account for the extraction, addition, deletion, preservation, storage, authenticity, and reliability of digital evidence, and prioritize digital evidence in inadmissibility and appraisal or weight of evidence. (Dr. Ghuffran Ahmed 2022).

METHODOLOGY

This research study is based on qualitative research methodology which focuses on gaining of depth understanding of subjective experiences. The data collected for this topic has been from different journals, books, articles, and research papers through the internet. In other words, the collection of data is from a secondary source. Due to this it gives a depth literature review and develops a conceptual model of the e-courts of Pakistan which very well describes the role of the judiciary, the common man, the online proceedings, and the implementation of the online decided decisions.

DISCUSSION AND ANALYSIS

Are the people of Pakistan aware of the E-court system?

In Pakistan's courts, awareness of the e-court system and digital technology is still in its infancy. The National Judicial Academy conducted a survey in 2021 and found that only 15% of Pakistanis had utilized the e-court system and 30% were aware of it. In addition, the survey revealed that only 20% of Pakistanis were aware of the use of video links and other cutting-edge technology in court. These figures suggest that people in Pakistan are still not very aware of e-courts and digital technology. This could be caused by several things, including, Inaccessibility to technology: The World Bank estimates that only 20% of Pakistanis have internet access, and 10% own smartphones. As a result, many people lack access to e-courts and other digital services. Inadequate awareness of the advantages of digital technology and e-courts. Many people are unaware of the ways these technologies can speed up the process of getting their cases heard and make access to justice easier. They might also be worried about how safe their personal information is or how trustworthy digital evidence is. Government investment is insufficient, E-courts and digital technology have not received significant investment from Pakistan's government. This has restricted the accessibility of these advancements and has made it hard for courts to advance their utilization. This proposes that there is an absence of consciousness of the capability of these innovations to make the equity framework more proficient and open. Video links can be used to allow witnesses to testify from afar, saving both the courts and the witnesses money and time. They can also be used to let people who have been harmed by a crime testify without having to be there in person, which can help people who have been traumatized by their experiences. The justice system's effectiveness can also be enhanced by making use of other cutting-edge tools like case management software and electronic filing systems. Judges, lawyers, and litigants can all communicate more easily with one another, and the court process can be streamlined with the help of these technologies. As to the use of current gadgets, for example, cell phones, tablets, or varying media hardware, for proof creation in Pakistani courts, there has been some advancement. The admissibility of electronic evidence, such as documents, images, videos, and audio recordings, has been acknowledged by courts. However, there may be a relatively low level of public awareness of the specific guidelines and procedures for submitting electronic evidence. Judges and lawyers, for example, are more likely to be familiar with the technical aspects of electronic evidence and whether or not it can be used in court. Despite this, efforts are being made to inform stakeholders, including the general public, about the procedures and requirements for presenting electronic evidence in court. To further enhance awareness and utilization of E-Court systems, video links for producing evidence, and modern devices in legal proceedings, it is crucial to invest in public awareness campaigns and educational initiatives. The dissemination of information regarding the benefits and procedures associated with these digital advancements can help bridge the knowledge gap among the public. Additionally, providing training programs and capacity-building initiatives for legal professionals, court staff, and other stakeholders will ensure a smoother transition towards a more technologically driven justice system in Pakistan.

The standards of Pakistan's E-Court system as compared to other countries.

Nations worldwide have acknowledged the importance of ensuring the uninterrupted and efficient functioning of their judicial systems, as they play a crucial role in upholding stability, order, and accountability, particularly in times of uncertainty. An option that emerges as a potential solution to this challenge is the implementation of online court proceedings. Although developing countries like Pakistan may encounter certain obstacles when it comes to conducting comprehensive legal procedures involving the recording of evidence and cross-examinations in this context, these extraordinary circumstances make it imperative to embrace such technological advancements. The notion of conducting court proceedings through online platforms is not entirely unprecedented within the jurisdiction of Pakistan. In May 2019, a tripartite panel of the Supreme Court presided over by the former Chief Justice Asif Saeed Khosa, formally inaugurated the commencement of litigation activities via the e-court system at the principal seat in Islamabad and the Karachi registry of the Supreme Court. In this regard, legal practitioners in Karachi efficaciously advocated their cases through videoconferencing, while the Supreme Court bench diligently adjudicated upon and pronounced judgments in the respective matters.

Furthermore, it is worth noting that overseas courts operating within the territorial ambit of Pakistan also employ virtual appearances when litigants are domiciled outside the geographical confines of the nation and are unable to personally attend court hearings. Considering the ongoing Covid-19 pandemic, the Lahore High Court has established a prototype court that adheres to the principles of social distancing while conducting legal proceedings. Notwithstanding these initial endeavors, substantial measures must be undertaken to advance toward a comprehensive and operational online court system. It is imperative to establish a streamlined mechanism for the electronic submission of court applications, the uploading of pertinent documents and attachments, the utilization of digital signatures, the improved utilization of electronic stamps (e-stamps), and the implementation of a comprehensive framework for conducting online legal arguments. Several nations, including the United States (US), Canada, and Turkey, have taken significant strides in establishing an online court system. Turkey, for instance, has implemented a comprehensive electronic platform that spans across all aspects of its judicial operations. Attorneys and citizens can review case files, make application payments, submit documents and claims, and file cases electronically in any court within the country. As a case progresses, parties involved can access relevant information and stay informed about the designated trial date without the need to personally contact court staff or rely on phone communication. In the United Kingdom (UK), the Supreme Court has adapted to the lockdown situation by conducting entire cases through video conferencing, marking a historic shift in its operations. In the US, the approach to online courts varies from state to state. In New York state, for example, Chief Judge DiFiore has postponed nonessential court functions and implemented a virtual court system to ensure continuity of proceedings. Furthermore, Countries like Malaysia, India, and Azerbaijan have successfully implemented and operationalized the E-court system, which continues to enhance its functionality over time. Many jurisdictions have already embraced the paperless judiciary model of the E-court, with Malaysia leading the way by establishing a fully functional E-court system that utilizes various components such as video conferencing, community and advocate portal systems, case management systems, court recording, and transcription systems. The E-court system facilitates the electronic transmission and receipt of documents, enables the online payment of filing fees, allows for the receipt of court notices, and facilitates the retrieval of court-related information. Pakistan's E-Court system is not fully advanced as compared to the above-mentioned countries, Pakistan's E-Court system was launched during covid-19 before this there is no future framework for launching an e-court unlike Malaysia launched in 2009. On the other hand, the United States of America normally used videoconferencing to record the testimonies of witnesses in the trial of *Johnny Deep v. Amber Heard[1]* Multiple testimonies were recorded through video link. Similarly, in Pakistan, the supreme court of Pakistan allowed cross-examination through video links in the case of *Meesha Shafi V. Ali Zafar*. Although the implementation of online courts may present significant challenges to the courts in Pakistan, the adoption of such a system holds the potential for substantial long-term benefits to our conventional court system. Introducing an online court system could significantly enhance access to justice for individuals residing in remote areas, particularly vulnerable minority groups, and women. Moreover, it has the potential to streamline court proceedings and potentially alleviate the persistent issue of case backlogs. Despite the formidable nature of this endeavor, initiating the process of digitalizing our courts is essential and must commence from a certain starting point.

Effect of E-Court on Litigation.

The Pakistan judiciary faced many problems in the litigation, on March 30, 2023, National Assembly was informed by the Minister of State on Law and Justice Mr. Shahadat Hussain. The

---

[1] Depp v. Heard, No. CL-2019-2911 (Va. Cir. Ct. Jul. 25, 2019).

house was informed regarding the pendency of the cases in Pakistan. In the past five years, it has been revealed that a significant number of cases remained unresolved in various superior courts in Pakistan. The statistics indicate that 1,861,616 cases were left unaddressed during this period. Specifically, there were 380,436 pending cases in 2022, 389,392 in 2021, 377,900 in 2020, 365,945 in 2019, and 347,947 in 2018. Additionally, the Supreme Court alone accounted for 239,595 delayed cases, with 51,744 in 2022, 51,766 in 2021, 46,516 in 2020, 42,582 in 2019, and 40,987 in 2018. There are multiples reason behind this first take into consideration that Pakistan's apex, as well as inferior courts, face pendency of cases due to a shortage of judges and court staff across the country. Secondly, problems arise regarding litigation therefore by installing digital technology in courts the number of pending cases will easily curtail. E-Court has had a significant impact on expediting the trial of pending cases in Pakistan, contributing to the goal of speedy justice. Online courts have streamlined case management and reduced litigation process delays by utilizing digital platforms and automation. Courts can better prioritize pending cases and monitor their progress with effective case management tools. This ensures that cases are resolved promptly. Additionally, a significant benefit of E-Court has been its capacity for remote hearings. Online platforms have made it possible for litigants, judges, and lawyers to participate in court proceedings from wherever they are by removing the requirement to be physically present in the courtroom. This has made it easier to continue legal proceedings and prevented disruptions caused by situations like the COVID-19 pandemic. Through distant hearings, forthcoming cases can be heard and settled without huge postponements. In addition, effective communication channels have been established by E-Court systems to facilitate the speedy trial of pending cases. Legal counselors can electronically record archives, submit applications, and speak with the court and restrict gatherings through the web-based entryway. Paperwork is reduced, information is shared more quickly, and unnecessary delays are avoided through this simplified communication method. Additionally, lawyers are provided with timely notifications and updates regarding case developments, allowing them to better prepare for and respond to cases. The timely progress of pending cases is facilitated by this effective communication, ensuring that they are resolved without undue delay. The implementation of digital record-keeping by E-Court systems, in addition to streamlining communication, significantly speeds up the trial of pending cases. Courts can quickly retrieve necessary documents and reduce their reliance on physical files by digitizing case records. Electronic access to case files eliminates delays caused by manual searching and handling of physical records for judges, lawyers, and court staff. This computerized record-keeping guarantees that case-related data is promptly available, supporting the fast preliminary of forthcoming cases. Additionally, sensitive data integrity and confidentiality are safeguarded by E-Court systems' secure access measures. Only authorized individuals, like lawyers, can access case-related documents and information by using secure login credentials and authentication protocols. E-Court systems use data encryption to protect sensitive information during transmission and storage in order to safeguard legal professionals. Data exchanged between lawyers, clients, and the court is protected from unauthorized access and interception thanks to encryption. Additionally, access to specific information is restricted based on the user's role and responsibilities using role-based access control mechanisms. An additional layer of protection for legal professionals is provided by these measures, which prevent unauthorized individuals from viewing or altering confidential case information. Additionally, protocols are frequently in place in online courts to safeguard the confidentiality of particular case details or proceedings. By sealing or redacting sensitive information from public access, confidential information is protected throughout the litigation process, protecting the interests of legal professionals and their clients. Moreover, online courts can possibly essentially diminish the expense of a court preliminary. Travel expenses, court costs, and fees for legal representation are just a few of the costs associated with traditional litigation. E-Court diminishes a large number of these costs by wiping out the requirement for actual presence in court, lessening travel costs, and improving on the documentation system. It likewise decreases the weight on the court framework, prompting cost reserve funds over the long haul. The speed with which cases can be resolved is one of the most significant advantages of E-Court. Due to the backlog of cases, procedural complexities, and limited court resources, traditional litigation frequently experiences delays. E-Court resolves these issues via mechanizing processes, smoothing out cases on the board, and furnishing decisions with advanced instruments for productive direction. As a result, cases can be processed and resolved more swiftly, leading to speedier justice.

Is The E-court system in Pakistan suitable for all types of cases?

The e-court framework in Pakistan is a somewhat new drive that has been carried out in stages starting around 2019. The framework considers the electronic documenting of cases, the issuance of e-orders, and the direct videoconferencing hearings. Although the system is still adolescent, it has the potential to drastically change how justice is delivered in Pakistan. The e-court system functions effectively for many various types of situations, although it performs best in straightforward or urgent matters. For instance, the system may be used to manage instances involving traffic tickets, small-time larceny, and other infractions. The method can also be used for pre-trial hearings and other procedural procedures. But not every case is appropriate for the e-court system. For instance, cases that involve intricate legal issues or necessitate witness testimony are not suitable for the system. Additionally, cases involving confidential or sensitive information are not suitable for the system. The electronic court system has a number of advantages over the traditional one. First, the system works better. It is possible to file and process cases more quickly, and parties do not need to travel to court for hearings. Second, the framework is more available. The system is accessible from any location with an internet connection, even for those who live in remote areas or have difficulty traveling. Thirdly, there is more openness in the system. All court archives and procedures are accessible on the web, which makes it more straightforward for people in general to follow the advancement of their cases. The e-court framework is still a work in progress, yet it can possibly change how equity is conveyed in Pakistan. A more just and equitable society may result from the system's contribution to enhancing the court system's efficiency, accessibility, and transparency. Here are a few explicit instances of how the e-court framework can be utilized in various sorts of cases: The defendant can plead guilty and pay the fine online in a traffic ticket case. The defendant can schedule a hearing online and participate in the hearing via videoconference if they wish to contest the ticket. The defendant can be arraigned and enter a plea online in a petty theft case. Online sentencing is available if the defendant is found guilty. The parties can exchange documents and motions online during a pre-trial hearing. By videoconference, they can also participate in the hearing. The parties can present their evidence online during a trial. Additionally, they can participate in the trial through videoconference. There are difficulties with the e-court system. The parties involved must possess a certain level of technical literacy, which presents a challenge. Another test is that guaranteeing the security of delicate information can be troublesome. The advantages of the e-court system outweigh the risks, and these difficulties are manageable. In general, the e-court system is a promising new innovation that has the potential to enhance Pakistan's legal system. The framework is still a work in progress, yet it emphatically affects how equity is conveyed in the country. As the framework keeps on developing, it is probably going to turn out to be much more effective, open, and straightforward.

Is Pakistan`s E-court system a biased way of availing justice?

The complex question of whether the e-court system is a biased method of obtaining justice has been the subject of much discussion. Some contend that the framework is innately one-sided for the people who approach innovation and the web. They point out that paying for the necessary hardware and software can be costly and that the system can be difficult to use for those who are not tech-savvy. They also say that the system can lead to a digital divide, making it harder for people who don't have access to the internet to get justice. Others make the case that the e-court system is superior to the traditional court system in terms of impartiality. They emphasize that the system eliminates the requirement for litigants and judges to meet in person, which may reduce the likelihood of bias. Additionally, they argue that the system facilitates judges' access to and consideration of all relevant evidence in a case, resulting in more impartial and just verdicts. At last, whether the e-court framework is a one-sided approach to profiting equity is an inquiry that must be responded to by observational exploration. Notwithstanding, it means quite a bit to take note that the framework is still a work in progress and that there are a few protections set up to forestall predisposition. For instance, the framework expects that all gatherings to a case approach a legal counselor and that everything proof is introduced in a fair and unprejudiced way. The Pakistani e-court system faces a number of other issues in addition to the possibility of bias. These difficulties include:

> - The judges and litigants lack of technical knowledge.
> - The high cost of the system's installation and upkeep.
> - The safety of confidential data.
> - The likelihood of cybercrime.

Regardless of these difficulties, the e-court framework in Pakistan can possibly be a significant device for conveying equity. A more just and equitable society may result from the system's contribution to enhancing the court system's efficiency, accessibility, and transparency. However, in order to guarantee that the system is utilized in an equitable and efficient manner, it is essential to address the obstacles it faces. Here are a few explicit instances of how the e-court framework can be one-sided. A prosecutor who isn't educated may experience issues documenting a case on the web or taking part in a videoconference hearing. A litigant may have difficulty gaining access to justice if they are unable to afford the software and hardware required. A disputant who lives in a distant region with an unfortunate web network might experience issues getting to the e-court framework. An unfamiliar judge may be more prone to err or have prejudice towards plaintiffs who use the e-court system. It is important to remember that these are only hypothetical biases in the electronic court system. The technology is still being developed, and there are several protections in place to prevent prejudice. But it's crucial to be aware of the possibility of prejudice and take action to lessen it.

Is the weightage of pros more over the cons of the E-court system in Pakistan?

Numerous benefits have resulted from Pakistan's adoption of the E-court system, which far exceed any negative effects. The use of technology in the legal system has greatly improved accessibility, efficiency, and transparency, transforming the field of law. The quick resolution of cases is one of the E-court system's main benefits. The time and effort needed for filing, paperwork, and case management have decreased because of the digitization of court proceedings. Electronic filing systems allow papers to be submitted and retrieved remotely, doing away with the requirement for physical presence and cutting down on delays brought on by human processing. The E-court system also encourages legal procedure openness. All parties, including litigants, attorneys, and judges, will have access to accurate and current information thanks to the digitalization of case files. This openness encourages public confidence in the court and makes it easier to administer justice in a fair and unbiased manner. E-court technology also improves access to justice. Geographical limitations and distance are no longer significant constraints because everyone with an internet connection may take part in judicial proceedings. Marginalized groups, distant locations, and those with physical limitations gain from this inclusion since they may now participate in judicial proceedings without having to pay high travel expenses or overcome difficult physical obstacles. The preservation of case files is ensured via electronic storage and retrieval, which also lowers the possibility of loss or damage. Additionally, digital archives make it simple to search for and retrieve information, facilitating quick access to earlier verdicts and legal precedents. This easy access to earlier rulings improves decision-making consistency and fosters legal clarity. The E-court system has a lot to offer in terms of cost effectiveness. Physical infrastructure, such as sizable courtrooms and storage facilities, is no longer required as a result of process digitization. This results in financial savings for both plaintiffs and the judicial system. Additionally, the electronic exchange of papers lowers printing and courier costs, which lowers overall costs for all parties. But it's important to be aware of some potential E-court system flaws. The digital gap, which refers to the inequality in access to technology and digital literacy among various social groups, is one such issue. Making sure that everyone, particularly those from economically disadvantaged backgrounds, has fair access to the tools they need to participate successfully in electronic court proceedings is vital. The integrity and security of electronic data provide another difficulty. Strong cybersecurity measures must be in place to guard against unauthorized access, data breaches, or manipulation given the sensitive nature of court processes and the confidential information involved. To adequately inform judges, attorneys, and court employees about data protection and privacy, training and awareness campaigns are also necessary.

DIGITAL EVIDENCE AND QAN00N-E-SHAHDHAT ORDER

Pakistan recognizes online hearings and cross-examination in 2019. The court recorded evidence and testimonies through video links on certain applications like Skype, Imo, Viber, WhatsApp, Zoom meetings, and many other applications. To reduce the burden of the pendency of the cases the worthy High Court of Peshawar decided multiples petition in a single judgment through online hearings in the case of *Muhammad Israr v. The State*[2]. The question brought before the court that Can the Court legally record the testimony of prosecution witnesses in criminal trials using various modern devices and applications such as video calls, Viber, Skype, IMO, WhatsApp, Facebook Messenger, Line Caller, and Video Conference? If so, would such statements be considered lawful according to Section 353 of the Code of Criminal Procedure 1898, which states that all evidence taken under Chapters XX, XXI, XXII, and XXII-A should be taken in the presence of the accused unless specifically stated otherwise? Furthermore, what would be the admissibility of such evidence under the provisions of the Qanun-e-Shahadat Order, 1984, especially Article 164? The prosecution requested the submission of proof. Due to PW Saeed Ullah's presence in Saudi Arabia for educational purposes, his statement was documented by the knowledgeable trial court through a video communication platform called IMO. During the cross-examination, the aforementioned PW acknowledged being in his residential room in Saudi Arabia while his statement was being recorded. Likewise, in related instances, the statement of Faisal Khan, the complainant, and an eyewitness, was recorded via a video call from Dubai. Moreover, the E-Court also includes the modern device and electronic evidence in the court which is normally understood as digital evidence. Pakistan's legal framework recognizes the admissibility of digital evidence through contemporary technological devices, as addressed in Articles 59 and 164. Within the framework of the Qanoon-e-Shahadat Order (QSO), Article 46-A establishes the relevance of digital evidence derived or stored through mechanical processes. This article complements another QSO provision stipulating that evidence may only be presented regarding facts in question or pertinent facts. Additionally, Article 73 of the QSO has been expanded to include electronic documents as primary evidence. In the case of *Mian Khalid Pervaiz v the STATE*[3]. The Supreme Court ruled that documentary evidence considered digital evidence, is admissible under Article 164 of the Qanoon-e-Shahadat Order 1984, Article 46-A, and 78-A of the Qanoon-e-Shahadat Order, along with the provisions of the Electronic Transactional Ordinance 2002. These legal

---

[2] Cr.. A.. No..1143--P//2019.
[3] 2021 SCMR 522.

provisions establish the procedure for the acceptance and validation of such documentary evidence. Similarly, in the case of **Shoaib Ahmad vs. State**[4] heard by the Gilgit-Baltistan Chief Court, the admissibility of evidence obtained from modern devices under Article 164 of the Qanoon-e-Shahadat Order was acknowledged. In this case, the crime was detected through CCTV footage, leading to the arrest of the accused. While Article 73 designates electronic documents as primary evidence, it can be argued that the article pertains more specifically to computer-generated information rather than computer-stored information, as additional copies can be made from stored information. Nevertheless, judicial interpretation is necessary, as evidenced by a recent ruling by LHC Judge Mr. Shahid Kareem, who declared that electronic documents should be treated as primary evidence subject to cross-examination. Furthermore, international standards exist for the admission of electronic evidence, emphasizing criteria such as authenticity, reliability, and admissibility. Meeting these standards requires establishing a chain of custody to ensure that the evidence remains unaltered and intact during the collection process. The inclusion of Article 164 in the Qanoon-e-Shahadat Order, 1984 addresses the presentation of evidence made accessible through modern devices. It grants the court the authority to allow the production of available evidence obtained via modern devices and technology if deemed appropriate. Efficient modern services have been hindered by legislative and procedural obstacles due to their reliance on electronic means of service and communication. Challenges such as unsigned and unattested documentation have created uncertainties regarding execution. Despite the uncertainties associated with unsigned evidence obtained through electronic devices under the Electronic Transactions Ordinance, some of these legal hurdles have been addressed by the legislation enacted in 2002. With its implementation, the Electronic Transactions Ordinance has become an integral part of the Qanoon-e-Shahadat Order, 1984, as defined in Article 2 (e). The utilization of contemporary devices for the purpose of presenting evidence has been found to be beneficial and demonstrated its efficacy in legal proceedings subsequent to the modifications made to the clauses of Qanun-e-Shahadat Order 1984 and the establishment of the Electronic Certification Accreditation Council (ECAC) under Section 18 of the Electronic Transaction Ordinance, 2002 (ETO). The ECAC, an independent entity operating under the Ministry of Information Technology & Telecom (MoIT), was created by the Federal Government of Pakistan. Numerous cases have been successfully resolved by relying on evidence obtained through modern technological means, which would have posed challenges if traditional methods were employed. The utilization of digital evidence in criminal cases has been significantly influenced by the Superior Courts in Pakistan. In a case titled *The State vs. Ahmed Omar Sheikh*[5], the Supreme Court of Pakistan established that video evidence holds significant value, but it can only be admissible in a court of law if certain conditions are fulfilled. These conditions include providing an explanation of how the video was obtained and its origin or source, as well as presenting a forensic report to demonstrate that the video has not been tampered with. Without meeting these requirements, video evidence lacks probative value. While mobile SMS is generally considered a relatively weak form of evidence in legal

---

[4] 2019 PCRLJ 57
[5] 2021 SCMR 873

proceedings, the Lahore High Court introduced a new rule in the case of *Shafqat Masih vs. The State*[6]. Under Article 164 of the Qanun-e-Shahadat Order 1984, SMS records are deemed to be strong evidence. Such evidence is considered primary evidence, allowing the court to make judgments based on it. Furthermore, in the case of *Shoaib Ahmad vs. State*, heard by the Gilgit-Baltistan Chief Court, evidence obtained under Article 164 of the Qanun-e-Shahadat Order was admitted. Similarly, in the case of *Salman Ahmad Khan vs. Judge Family Court, Multan*[7], the Lahore High Court addressed the dissolution of marriage issue, wherein video recordings were presented as modern evidence to demonstrate the husband's mistreatment of his wife. Although Article 164 of the Qanun-e-Shahadat Order 1984 was not strictly applicable in the family court, the court deemed it acceptable to receive such evidence. Hence, in family court proceedings, modern device evidence is also considered, subject to verification and inquiry procedures. In the case of *Sadaqat Ullah Khan vs. The State*, the Lahore High Court resolved a matter involving reckless driving and disregarding traffic signals, wherein evidence in the form of modern means was obtained.

BARRIERS AND SOLUTIONS

The implementation of E-Court systems and online proceedings with the integration of digital evidence in Pakistan faces several barriers that must be addressed to ensure the smooth functioning and effectiveness of the legal system.

The digital divide is one of the main obstacles. Similar to many other nations, Pakistan has unequal access to technology and levels of digital literacy. Many people, especially those from economically poor families or rural locations, do not have the tools and knowledge needed to engage in online proceedings in a meaningful way. This gap prevents everyone from having access to justice and makes it difficult to adopt E-Court systems. To get over this obstacle, efforts must be taken to close the digital divide by giving underprivileged populations access to technological infrastructure, internet connectivity, and digital literacy initiatives. The validity and veracity of digital evidence are a big hurdle as well. The integrity and admissibility of digital evidence must be shown in order for it to be accepted in court. There may be questions about the reliability, falsification, or modification of digital evidence. Strong cybersecurity measures must be put in place to guarantee the security and integrity of digital evidence in order to allay these worries. Encryption, safe storage methods, and rigorous access restrictions are some examples of this. The reliability and acceptability of digital evidence in courts can also be improved by creating a framework for digital forensics and certifying agencies. Another difficulty is the incompatibility of various E-Court systems and technology frameworks. Inconsistencies in the technology and

---

[6] 2021 MLD 1415.
[7] PLD 2017 Lah 698.

software employed by various courts and legal organizations might obstruct effective data exchange, collaboration, and communication. Standardization of technological infrastructure, software platforms, and data formats is essential to ensure interoperability among E-Court systems and facilitate the exchange of information and evidence. Legal and regulatory barriers also need to be addressed. The existing legal framework in Pakistan may not adequately address the unique challenges and requirements of E-Court systems and online proceedings. It is crucial to enact comprehensive legislation that explicitly recognizes the legal validity and admissibility of digital evidence, defines the procedures for its collection, preservation, and presentation in court, and establishes rules for online proceedings. Clear guidelines regarding the authentication and certification of digital evidence are essential to provide a solid foundation for the use of technology in the legal system. Solutions for E-Court and Online Proceedings with Digital Evidence in Pakistan to overcome the barriers discussed above, several solutions can be implemented.

Infrastructure Growth For the effective adoption of E-Court systems and online processes, it is essential to have a solid and dependable technical infrastructure, including high-speed internet access and sufficient hardware resources. Underserved areas and underprivileged groups should receive priority in infrastructure investments. To improve the technology knowledge and abilities of legal practitioners, judges, court personnel, and litigants, comprehensive digital literacy programs should be put into place. Individuals can benefit from these workshops by learning how to use E-Court technologies, appreciating the value of digital evidence, and effectively participating in online proceedings. To safeguard the integrity and confidentiality of digital evidence, it is crucial to implement strong cybersecurity measures, such as encryption, secure storage systems, and access restrictions. The development of digital forensics teams and collaboration with cybersecurity professionals can improve the validity and acceptability of digital evidence. To maintain compatibility and interoperability among E-Court systems, standards for technological infrastructure, software platforms, and data formats should be developed. Collaboration, data interchange, and smooth communication between various courts and legal institutions would be made possible by this. Enacting comprehensive legislation that addresses the unique challenges and requirements of E-Court systems and online proceedings is crucial. The legal framework should explicitly recognize the legal validity and admissibility of digital evidence, define procedures for its collection and presentation, and establish rules for online proceedings. Collaboration with legal experts and stakeholders can aid in drafting effective legislation.

POLICY PROPOSAL AND RECOMMENDATION

The following recommendations aim for the betterment of the e-court system in Pakistan:

1. Establish rules and regulations regarding custody, storage, authenticity, and reliability of digital proceeding documents and availed digital evidence.

2. Install the Court Management System (CMS) in the courts whose data excess is restricted to the competent authorities.

3. Appoint an expert in the digital world to assist the court in analyzing digital evidence presented by the parties.

4. In each district, an expert team should be prepared to account for the extraction, addition, deletion, preservation, storage, authenticity, and reliability of digital evidence and other proceeding documents.

5. Updated versions of hardware and software and high-speed internet should be provided in the courts including video conferencing equipment and data management systems.

6. On the orders of the Court a competent authority like BS-17 grade and above Assistant Commissioner of the zone should be present at the online hearing, taking an oath and signature. This person is a witness to the hearing and may face termination if found biased.

7. In the scenario where any of the parties is residing in a foreign and is availing the online proceeding facility of Pakistan, it should take place in the presence of any competitive authority officer of the Pakistani Embassy. It should be made mandatory that the officer should take the oath and sign and act as a witness to the hearing. If found biased strict actions are to be taken against him.

8. Judges, lawyers, and the other court staff of each district should be provided with mandatory training sessions regarding the usage of the e-court system as every person does not pertain the same experience and knowledge regarding the ICT and after the training, a test should be conducted to evaluate their skills regarding it.

9. An Application should be developed like the tax asaan applications collaborated with the Nadra through which the oath can be taken and the party's identity and other relevant information can be verified with the help of fingerprints.

10. The e-court system should be spread all across the country not specifically in the main cities as issues arise in every part of the country, not particularly in the main cities so the need for an e-court system is in both rural and urban areas. Perhaps there are more unresolved issues in the rural areas as access to avail justice is an impossible reach so fulfilling the need of this facility in those areas is mandatory.

11. The training and the test regarding it should be made mandatory like the LAW-GAT test to qualify as a lawyer for the newcomers as well as previous practitioners.

CONCLUSION

The increasing population in Pakistan has led to a rise in cases to be adjudicated, and the nature of disputes and the availability of litigants and witnesses remain issues. Information and communications technology has created a new era of accessible, speedy, and continuous justice through the E-Court system. Digital transformation of the court system is crucial for making justice universal, portable, and available, boosting investor confidence and the economy. To revolutionize the judicial system in Pakistan, it is essential to examine available technology and adopt the most cost-effective and quality-added technology. Establishing E-courts in the current judicial structure can reduce the backlog of cases, enable litigants to file cases online, facilitate vulnerable groups, and relieve aggrieved individuals. However, the E-court initiative has only one facility, a video link, and lacks proper implementation and awareness among judges, lawyers, and judicial officers. The future of the online court raises complex concerns, but the advantages outweigh the disadvantages. A desirable model should initially be based on simple, low-cost procedures, and be adopted as an experimental program. The trailblazing of a new legal model should be carefully done, accommodating the existing legal system in a controlled and systematic environment to increase the accessibility of justice.

In conclusion, the lessons learned from the online court system can improve the legal system and minimize future conflicts.

References

. Dr. Muhammad Asif Khan, A. P. (2021). Electronic Court System and Speedy Justice: A Comparative Critical Analysis of Legal Systems in Pakistan, Malaysia, and India. *Journal of Law and Social Policy*, 25.

Abida Naureen, A. (2023, January 11). *E-Court System: a Dire Need*. Retrieved from Daily Times : https://dailytimes.com.pk/1049864/e-court-system-a-dire-need/

Ballesteros, T. (2021). International Perspectives on Online Dispute Resolution in the E-Commerce Landscape. *International Journal of Online Dispute Resolution*, 15.

Bashir, S. (2020, December 02). *Judge hears cases online from quarantine*. Retrieved from The Tribune : https://tribune.com.pk/story/2274308/judge-hears-cases-online-from-quarantine

Dr Tariq Mahmood, T. C. (2020, April 30). *Efficient Justice: Benefits of E-technologies in Courts/ADR in Pakistan*. Retrieved from Courting the Law: https://courtingthelaw.com/2020/04/30/commentary/efficient-justice-benefits-of-e-technologies-in-courts-adr-in-pakistan/

DR. GHUFRAN AHMED, K. M. (2022, september). *DIGITAL EVIDENCE AND THE ADMINISTRATION OF CRIMINAL JUSTICE*. Retrieved from Blackstone Law Journal: https://www.bsolpk.org/digital-evidence-and-the-administration-of-criminal-justice#_ftnref7

Georgia Harley, A. S. (2018, January 22). *E-justice: does electronic court reporting improve court performance?* Retrieved from World Bank Blogs : https://blogs.worldbank.org/europeandcentralasia/e-justice-does-electronic-court-reporting-improve-court-performance

Hamid, A. (2020). The case for smart courts Digital transformation of. *RIAA Barker Gillette* , 4.

Jafri, A. (2022, APRIL 19). *Technology for better justice*. Retrieved from THE INTERNATIONAL NEWS : https://www.thenews.com.pk/amp/950767-technology-for-better-justice

Khilji, U. (2019, october 14). *Technology for Justice* . Retrieved from Dawn : https://www.dawn.com/news/1510741

Malik, H. (2021, April 11). *THE CASE FOR ONLINE HEARINGS*. Retrieved from The Tribune Magazine : https://tribune.com.pk/story/2294089/the-case-for-online-hearings

Qazi, M. (2023, April 11). *Infusing Digital Technology in Judicial Operations in Pakistan: A Critical Analysis of Global Best Practices and Local Initiatives*. Retrieved from SSRN : https://papers.ssrn.com/sol3/papers.cfm?abstract_id=4378378

Shahzad, S. (2020, May 13). *The case for online courts in Pakistan*. Retrieved from The Tribune : https://tribune.com.pk/article/96235/the-case-for-online-courts-in-pakistan

Zeeshan Ashraf Qureshi Ph.D. (Law) Scholar, S. o. (2021). The Conceptual Framework for Institutionalisation of E-court System in Pakistan. *Journal of Peace, Development and Communication*, 13.